Read All About

TRANSPORT

by Lucy Beevor

raintree

a Capstone company — publishers for children

Raintree is an imprint of Capstone Global Library Limited, a company incorporated in England and Wales having its registered office at 264 Banbury Road, Oxford, OX2 7DY – Registered company number: 6695582

www.raintree.co.uk
myorders@raintree.co.uk

Edited by Peter Mavrikis
Designed by Kayla Rossow
Original illustrations © Capstone Global Library Limited 2022
Picture research by Morgan Walters
Production by Laura Manthe
Originated by Capstone Global Library Ltd
Printed and bound in India

978 1 3982 2594 7 (hardback)
978 1 3982 2593 0 (paperback)

British Library Cataloguing in Publication Data
A full catalogue record for this book is available from the British Library.

Acknowledgements
We would like to thank the following for permission to reproduce photographs: Alamy: Michael Klinec, top 31, Xinhua, bottom 31; iStockphoto: dstephens, bottom 5; NASA, top 29; Shutterstock: Alex Luke Levy, top 19, Alexander Kirch, bottom 8, Alexander Oganezov, bottom 24, Andy Dean Photography, top 9, Angelo Giampiccolo, 10, ArnoudNL, bottom 20, Artsiom Petrushenka, 28, Aun Photographer, 4, Castleski, middle left 29, cate_89, 13, CHEN MIN CHUN, top 15, Dee Browning, bottom 19, Denis Belitsky, (plane) Cover, Dmitry Kalinovsky, top 23, Ekaterina Pokrovsky, (bicycles) Cover, Everett Collection, 14, Halfpoint, 1, top 8, horsemen, bottom 23, Hurst Photo, bottom 7, Ilia Platonov, bottom 16, Jemastock, design element throughout, jgorzynik, bottom 21, JHVEPhoto, top 16, Jim Lambert, top 26, Johnny Habell, bottom 25, kelly Shen, top 11, Kelvin Degree, design element throughout, lunamarina, 22, Mark and Anna Photography, top 20, Mike Brake, top 5, Mike Focus, bottom 11, Monkey Business Images, bottom 9, NAN728, bottom 12, Noel V. Baebler, top 24, noraismail, top 12, Philip Bird LRPS CPAGB, top 25, Piotr Zajac, bottom 26, PomInOz, top 17, rCarner, bottom 15, ReVelStockArt, design element throughout, Scharfsinn, 6, StockphotoVideo, top 27, stocksre, top 21, THINK A, bottom 17, Triff, bottom right 29, vaalaa, 18, VIKTOR GRISHCHENKO, middle 11, Vitpho, top 7, VLADYSLAV DANILIN, middle 5, Volodimir Zozulinskyi, 30, Wendy Kaveney Photography, bottom 27, white snow, (watercolor) Cover

Every effort has been made to contact copyright holders of material reproduced in this book. Any omissions will be rectified in subsequent printings if notice is given to the publisher.

Contents

Words in **bold** are in the glossary.

Chapter 1

What is transport?

Transport moves people and things from one place to another. It soars, floats, zooms and rolls. Fasten your seatbelt – let's find out more!

Giant container ships carry **cargo** across seas and oceans.

Fire engines are special vehicles. They take firefighters and their tools to fight fires.

Hot air balloons can float. A burner fills the balloon with hot air, which is lighter than cold air. Hot air makes the balloon go up!

Deep-sea **submersibles** help scientists explore the deepest parts of the ocean.

Chapter 2

On the road

We use transport with wheels every day. How many of these road vehicles have you spotted on your travels?

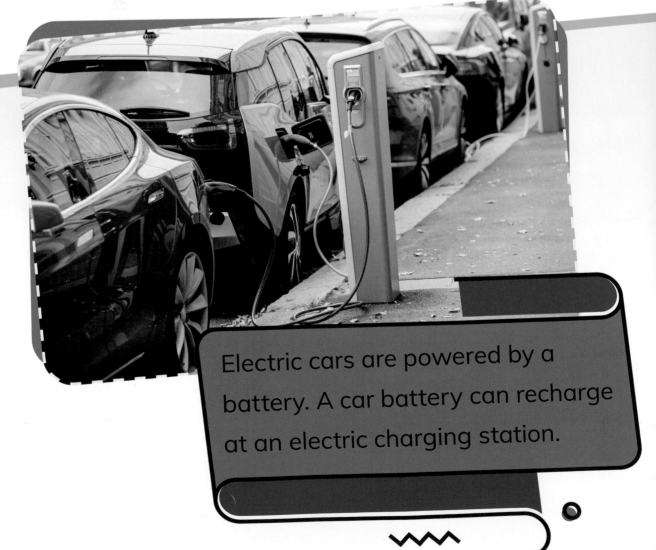

Electric cars are powered by a battery. A car battery can recharge at an electric charging station.

A lorry has two parts. The driver's cab and **engine** are at the front. The trailer is at the back.

trailer

cab

Some children travel to school in school buses.

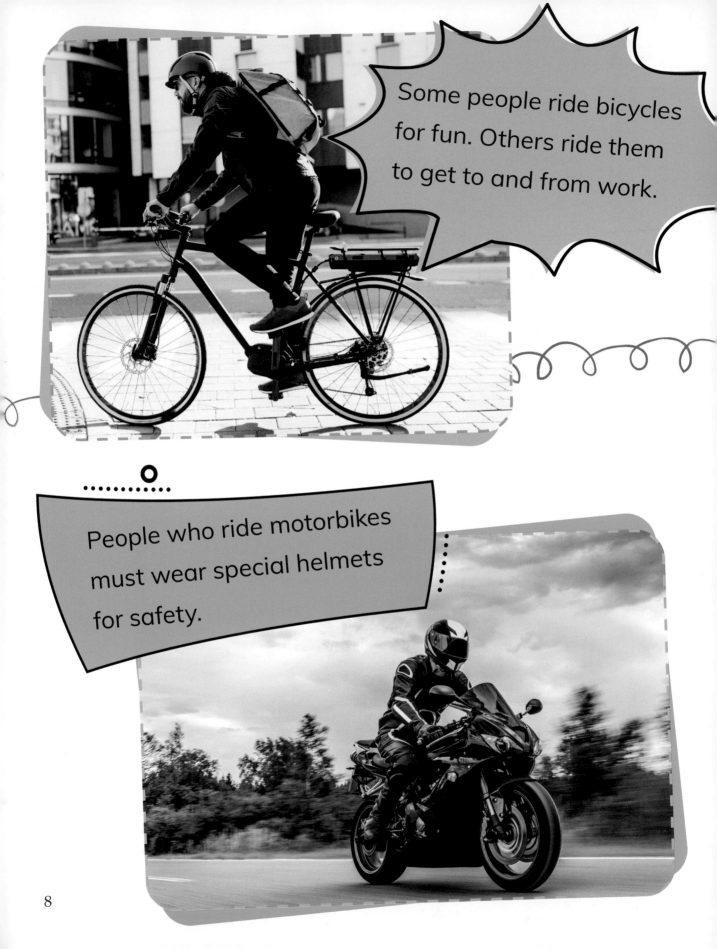

Some people ride bicycles for fun. Others ride them to get to and from work.

People who ride motorbikes must wear special helmets for safety.

8

Some families go on holiday in motorhomes or caravans. They have everything you need inside – even a toilet!

To make a scooter go, push off the ground with your foot!

9

Chapter 3

On water

Boats come in lots of shapes and sizes. But they all have one thing in common – they float on water!

The parts of a boat have special names. A hull is the boat's body. The front is called the bow. The back is called the stern.

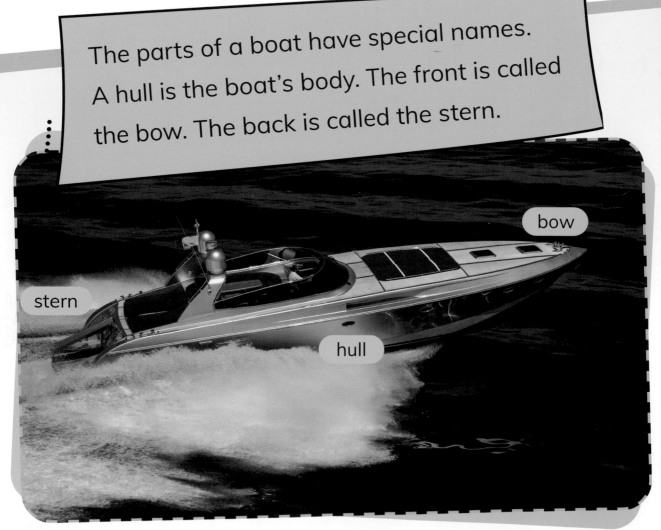

bow

stern

hull

Some boats are powered by a person. They row with an oar or a paddle.

Speed boats have a **propeller** and a fast engine.

Sailing boats have tall sails. Strong winds push against the sails and move the boat forwards.

Submarines can dive deeper than 240 m (800 feet). That's more than the length of two football pitches.

Cruise ships are floating hotels that take people on trips to different places.

tugboat

Tugboats are small and strong. They push or pull bigger boats in busy **ports**.

Chapter 4

On tracks

Trains zoom between stations on railway lines. But trains are not the only transport that runs on tracks. Hop on board to learn more!

The first trains were powered by steam made by burning coal. Now trains run on diesel or electricity.

steam engine

coal

Trains can carry lots of people. If more people take trains, there will be fewer cars and less **pollution**.

locomotive

goods van

Freight trains pull heavy cargo in goods vans. The engine at the front is a locomotive.

Underground trains zoom through tunnels below ground.

Imagine riding a "flying train"! This train carriage hangs below the track.

Trams are small, light trains that move people around cities on **rails**.

The fastest train in the world is the bullet train in China.

Chapter 5

In the air

Before people could fly in aeroplanes,
they could not easily visit faraway places.
Now, planes make travel easier and faster.

Aeroplanes have two wings, a tail
and one or more engines for flying.

The pilot sits in the cockpit and uses controls to fly the plane.

A seaplane has floats so it can take off from, and land on, water.

floats

Helicopters have spinning rotor blades to lift them off the ground. The tail rotor helps the helicopter fly in a straight line.

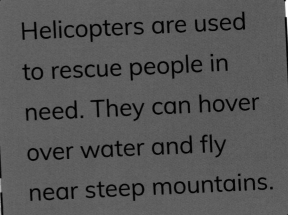

Helicopters are used to rescue people in need. They can hover over water and fly near steep mountains.

Stunt pilots perform daring twists, turns and rolls in the air.

The F-35B flies straight up and lands straight down. It can take off from the roof of a building or land on a ship!

Chapter 6

At work

Farm vehicles make a farmer's work easier.

Emergency vehicles help save people's lives.

What other types of vehicles have special jobs?

Farmers use tractors for moving crops in a trailer, pulling a plough and lifting heavy objects.

plough

Diggers have big buckets for scooping up soil.

Bulldozers clear rocks and rubble. Tracks stop them sinking into sand or soil.

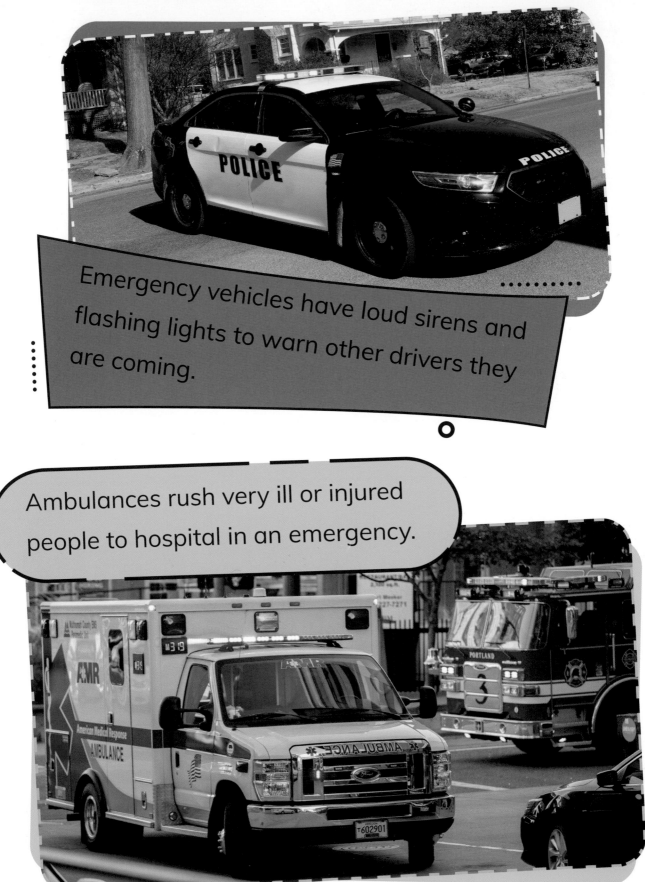

Emergency vehicles have loud sirens and flashing lights to warn other drivers they are coming.

Ambulances rush very ill or injured people to hospital in an emergency.

Rescue boats and their crews help people who are in danger at sea.

Bin lorries collect rubbish to take to the tip or recycling centre. The loader lifts the bin and tips out the rubbish into the trailer.

loader

Chapter 7

At play

Transport isn't just for moving people and things around. It can also be lots of fun!

A Segway is an electric scooter. To drive it, simply push the handlebars in the direction you want to go.

Monster trucks can do amazing stunts such as backflips and **wheelies**.

BMX bikes are light but sturdy – perfect for jumps, spins and slides!

Crowds of people cheer as racing cars zoom around a track.

Chapter 8

In space

Space is a very big place. We use special types of transport to help us explore deep space, the Moon and other planets.

rocket thrusters

orbiter

Astronauts used to fly in a space shuttle. When it was time to launch, two rockets shot the shuttle into space.

The SpaceX Dragon took astronauts to space in 2020. The Falcon 9 rocket sent it into space.

A Lunar Rover is a car for astronauts to drive on the Moon!

Scientists send rovers to other planets to search for water and other signs of life.

Chapter 9

Transport of the future

Inventors come up with new ideas for transport all the time.

The Hyperloop uses a floating "pod" to send **passengers** through a tube at very high speeds.

The Mercedes-Benz Future Bus uses computers and cameras to drive itself.

Flying taxis could whisk people through the air on quick journeys.

Glossary

cargo goods carried on a ship, train, plane or other vehicle

engine machine with moving parts that turns energy into power

passenger person who travels in a vehicle

pollution gas and smoke that are harmful to the world around us

port place where ships load or unload cargo or passengers

propeller blades spun by an engine to move a vehicle such as an aeroplane or boat

rails steel tracks that trains travel on

submersible sea vessel that operates underwater

wheelie trick where a vehicle balances on its back wheels

Index